LAMDA

CONTEMPORARY MONOLOGUES FOR YOUNG MEN AND WOMEN

Edited by Shaun McKenna

PUBLISHED BY
OBERON BOOKS
FOR THE LONDON ACADEMY OF
MUSIC AND DRAMATIC ART

First printed in 2000 in *Contemporary Speeches for Young Women* and *Contemporary Speeches for Young Men*.

This edition first published in 2004 for LAMDA Ltd.
by Oberon Books Ltd.
(incorporating Absolute Classics)
521 Caledonian Road, London N7 9RH
Tel: 0171 607 3637 / Fax: 0171 607 3629
e-mail: oberon.books@btinternet.com
www.oberonbooks.com

Compilation copyright © LAMDA Ltd. 2004

Contributions copyright © the contributors

LAMDA Ltd. is hereby identified as author of this compilation in accordance with section 77 of the Copyright, Designs and Patents Act 1988.

The contributors are hereby identified as authors of their contributions in accordance with section 77 of the Copyright, Designs and Patents Act 1988.

This book is sold subject to the condition that it shall not by way of trade or otherwise be circulated without the publisher's consent in any form of binding or cover or circulated electronically other than that in which it is published and without a similar condition including this condition being imposed on any subsequent purchaser.

A catalogue record for this book is available from the British Library.

ISBN 1 84002 424 0

Cover design: Society
Cover photograph: John Haynes

Printed in Great Britain by Antony Rowe Ltd, Chippenham.

Contents

PART ONE: TEENS

Female

Male

PART TWO: TWENTIES

Female

Male

Introduction

Contemporary Monologues for Young Men and Women contains a collection of speeches from plays written since 1985, suitable for both teenagers and young adults.

The collection, for ease of reference, has been divided into three sections, based on the age of the characters. Each extract has been specially selected for its effectiveness and coherence as a scene in isolation from the play in which it originates. Notes on the character's age, situation, and accent/dialect accompany each selection. The spelling and punctuation of the stage directions as well as the speeches themselves have been reproduced as they appeared in their original form. The date of the first performance or publication and the international standard book number have also been included.

Shaun McKenna

PART ONE: TEENS – FEMALE

Contents

Male

PART THREE: THIRTIES

Female

Male

Introduction

Contemporary Monologues for Young Men and Women contains a collection of speeches from plays written since 1985, suitable for both teenagers and young adults.

The collection, for ease of reference, has been divided into three sections, based on the age of the characters. Each extract has been specially selected for its effectiveness and coherence as a scene in isolation from the play in which it originates. Notes on the character's age, situation, and accent/dialect accompany each selection. The spelling and punctuation of the stage directions as well as the speeches themselves have been reproduced as they appeared in their original form. The date of the first performance or publication and the international standard book number have also been included.

Shaun McKenna

PART ONE: TEENS – FEMALE

THE CHAMPION OF PARIBANOU
by Alan Ayckbourn

The Champion of Paribanou was first performed at the Stephen Joseph Theatre in the Round, Scarborough in November 1996.

This play for children is set in the mythical and mystical East. It deals with questions of good and evil. Prince Ahmed is in love with Murganah, the vizier's tomboyish daughter. Princess Nouronnihar has been ordered by her father to marry Ahmed or one of his brothers. As none of them want the match, they have formed a plot to gain time. Each of the princes is to go on a quest to bring back a gift to Nouronnihar, which she will subsequently reject. Ahmed's quest leads him to the Mountain of Storms. Here he meets Paribanou, a young maiden, who tells him her story in the following speech.

Accent: any.

PARIBANOU: Sit down. We have much to talk about. But first I must explain a little. Do you like fairy tales, Ahmed?

Listen to this one. And pay attention. Once upon a time there were two children. A sister and a brother. Their mother had died when they were very young and as a result the brother's behaviour was often very wild. They were brought up by their father, a good and powerful wizard in the most happy of kingdoms. One day it happened that their father had to leave them in order to make a journey. He left them in the care of the servants and before he went he bade them to be good and well-behaved during his absence. If they were good, he said, when he returned he would reward them with wonderful gifts. And it happened that whilst he was away, although the daughter obeyed her father, the brother did not. Instead he meddled with his father's spell books and not only tormented his sister but was cruel to the servants. In fact, he became so wild and uncontrollable that when the father returned the palace was all but in ruins. For by then the son, in his search for wealth and power, had sold his very soul to Schaibar himself...

Schaibar, the Stranger from the Darkness who seeks to lead us all into that same Darkness. Anyway, the wizard could do nothing, realising he had lost his only son forever. And he became first sad and then angry with his daughter for just feebly standing by and doing nothing to stop her brother. And her punishment was to remain in a beautiful but lonely cave high on a mountain. A prison she could never leave until she learnt to stand up for what is right and to oppose all that is bad. Alone with only Nasuh for company. You are the first visitor this place has ever seen, Ahmed. Welcome.

Maybe you were sent? Who knows?

Available in *Alan Ayckbourn: Plays Two*, published by Faber & Faber Ltd. Reprinted by kind permission of the publisher.

ISBN: 0 571 19457 5

SEA URCHINS

by Sharman Macdonald

Sea Urchins was first produced at the Dundee Rep Theatre in May 1998, a co-production between the Tron Theatre Company and the Dundee Rep Theatre.

The play is set in the summer of 1961 on the wild Welsh coast. Rena, a Scottish girl of eleven, is on holiday with her family and struggling with the pains of growing up. She indulges in a fantasy correspondence with a multiple murderer, Manning, who is on the run from the police and whose story fills the newspapers. This speech is addressed to the (unseen) murderer and concerns a twelve-year-old girl, Noelle, whom Rena has met on the beach.

Accent: Scottish.

RENA: (*Whispers.*) Dear Mr Manning. Dear, dear, dear Mr Manning. I've a candidate for murder I want to introduce you to. I've got your number nine sitting in a fresh water stream in Wales waiting to have your knife plunge into her guts. Dear Mr Manning please don't take any other applications. This is important. Noelle Williams is the one for you. Please get yourself down here by the quickest method of travel. I'll reimburse any expenses you incur though it may take me a while. Girls can be bad bitches Mr Manning but Noelle Williams takes the biscuit. She'll make an awful woman when she comes to maturity. You'd be doing the world a favour were you to cease her being. About dinner time should suit. We'll all be gathered. You'll know the bitch by her yellow swimsuit and the rolls of fat on her upper arms. And the three necklace of Venus lines that circle her dark neck. She says they're a promise of the beauty that is to come. Don't go confusing the two of us. There's some maintain we look alike. I have no necklace of Venus round my neck as Noelle kindly pointed out last year. I have a red swimsuit, Mr Manning. Just so you know. It clashes with my hair but my mother says be brazen and be damned. She bought me the swimsuit. If only you were God, Mr Manning. If you were God I would ask you to let me sing so that I could join them. I'm all alone here Mr Manning. My Father would forgive me the guitar if

I could sing. Noelle can sing. And Rhiannon. I can hear it. I dream it, Mr Manning. I dream it so hard that when I wake up I can taste it. My own voice and it's lovely. Then I open up my mouth. And the sound that I hear. Mr Manning, it's an abomination. And it hurts my heart. Kill Noelle for me please. She only has to look at me. She knows all my misery. She knows it better than I do myself. That's not a thing any person should have to suffer. So you just kill her. We're all here on earth for a purpose. Your purpose is to rid the world of Noelle Williams and make me happy. No-one's all bad Mr Manning. You do this death for me. It'll be your good deed. It'll get you into Heaven.

Available in *Sea Urchins*, published by Faber & Faber Ltd. Reprinted by kind permission of the publisher.

ISBN: 0 571 19695 1

BOLD GIRLS

by Rona Munro

Bold Girls was commissioned by 7:84 Scottish People's Theatre and first performed at the Cumbernauld Theatre, Strathclyde in September 1990, subsequently touring widely.

The play is set in Belfast in 1990, against the background of the Troubles. Deirdre is fifteen, a disturbed young girl who has been hanging around outside the home of Marie Donnelly, a widow whose husband was killed by the British army. In this speech, Deirdre reveals why she has 'infiltrated' Marie's family. She believes Marie's late husband, Michael, to be her father, and that she was conceived during his marriage to Marie. Marie has just discovered that Michael had also been having an affair with her best friend, Cassie. Deirdre once saw Michael and Cassie making love in a car.

Accent: Belfast.

DEIRDRE: He was my Daddy.

He was. He was my Daddy.

My Mum told me.

She said my Dad was a bad man, and for years I thought my Daddy was a hood, then she told me he was a bad man because he left her, left her flat with me on the way and I thought that didn't make him bad because didn't I want to leave her too? So I started asking.

No-one will tell you the truth to your face. But I heard his name, so I went looking for him. I used to follow him about. That's how I saw him with her. In his car. She was wearing a bright red dress with no back to it, that made me stare first you know because I couldn't imagine how she could stand it being so cold, even in his car. Then they moved and I saw his face so I had to stay then, I had to stay and watch. I saw his face and I saw hers just before he kissed her… Just before he did she looked like my Granny, old and tired and like she didn't care about anything at all anymore…

I stopped following him after that. I thought if he was with her he'd never come back to me and my Mum. Then I heard he was dead…

Pause.

I didn't know where to look for him then. I'm cold. Can I get a cup of tea or something?

Available in *First Run 3: New Plays By New Writers*, selected and introduced by Matthew Lloyd and published by Nick Hern Books. Reprinted by kind permission of the publisher.

ISBN: 1 85459 059 6

PART ONE: TEENS – MALE

CROSSFIRE

by Michel Azama
(translated by Nigel Gearing)

Crossfire was first performed, in the original French, in Dijon in 1989. It was subsequently produced in the UK, in this translation, by Paines Plough in August 1993, at the Traverse Theatre Edinburgh and subsequently in London.

'Crossfire' is a powerful play about war. Characters are caught in the crossfire both literally and metaphorically, as the issues that war brings up impinge on their lives and relationships and they tumble through the checkpoint between life and death.

Yonathan is fifteen. He is a freedom fighter, in an unnamed struggle, who has just been killed by his former best friend, Ismail, circumstances having forced them to fight on opposite sides. He speaks to the audience.

Accent : any.

YONATHAN: The most difficult thing to do is cut the
    throat of a man who's still alive.

You mustn't waste a single slash of the knife and it's best
to do it from behind.

Playing the hero is pointless.

We've booby-trapped cars doors cigarette-packets
jerrycans stuffed with TNT we've fired fired fired even
on kids because they grow up one day
they'll shoot you in the back.

Helicopters dropped clusters of missiles
the camp burned the vines burned across miles of hills
stone-walls exploded.

It only takes 48 hours and then you're finished with the bombs the explosions the human pulp.

Hang on in there hang on in there just a bit further till the end
whole bunches of kids would throw themselves under the tanks they were crushed to death whole groups of them others set on fire with flame-throwers
human torches still running for another hundred yards.

All for one more second of life.

Blood filling your hands clothes eyes walls.

Slaughter slaughter slaughter.

KERPOW! The other guy falls you step over him you don't see anything any more you move forwards a corpse falls on top of you explodes into bits and pieces all cut to shreds and splashing you in a shower of blood.

At every step children in little bits babies their heads burst open
disembowelled women holding on to their children you're like an animal it's them or you
fire — bang! – at anything that moves a kid a cat a pal.

Bang bang bang save your skin bang bang bang bang.

He falls and does not move.

Available in *Crossfire*, published by Oberon Books Ltd. Reprinted by kind permission of the publisher.

ISBN: 1 870259 34 3

CROSSFIRE

by Michel Azama

See note on the play on page 23.

In this powerful play about the atrocity of war, fifteen-year-old Ismail and Yonathan have been inseparable friends. Now there is civil war, based on religion, and Yonathan is leaving to join the 'other side'. Ismail is talking to Yonathan.

Accent : any.

ISMAIL: Have you gone mad or what?

It's crazy. You were born here. We've always played soccer together. It's crazy.

No-one will hurt you here. You come from round here.

We're trapped. I feel lost. I try and understand what's going on. I listen to the radio. I try and keep up. This war's a war of lies. Everybody's lying. You can't know any more.

Wait. You can't just leave like that. We'll still see each other.

When we were kids the war was just a good excuse for bunking off school. You remember, we used to say: no school today! today's a bombing day!

You're my mate. My mate. One hundred per cent. I can't think of you as the enemy, it's impossible. I'd get killed for you here and now like a shot... Like a shot.

You remember you wanted to be a doctor and me an engineer.

On my fifteenth birthday we had a party, a picnic by the sea with some girls.

There haven't been any since.

Remember, that was the day it began.

For our picnic we had a barbecue. We danced with the girls. When we got back we didn't understand what that guy was saying. He was saying things are hotting up out there and when we got back...

I found my mother in tears. She thought I was dead.

We've spent our whole lives playing soccer and stealing figs.

You can't leave just like that. Over on the other side with the others. I don't believe you. Shooting at us. Shooting at me perhaps. I can't believe that.

You haven't a single real feeling in the whole of your body.

Available in *Crossfire*, published by Oberon Books Ltd. Reprinted by kind permission of the publisher.

ISBN: 1 870259 34 3

YO-YO

by Dino Mahoney

Yo-Yo was first performed at the Warehouse Theatre, Croydon in April 1995 and was the winner of the 1994 South London International Playwriting Festival.

Lego is a disturbed fourteen-year-old boy from London. The play is set in a downmarket guest house at a Cornish seaside resort, during the August bank holiday weekend. Lego is staying there with his mother, who has left him alone for the weekend. He meets Kevin, a divorced teacher, who is hoping to spend some time with his own son. Lego, bored and lonely, forces Kevin to pay him attention.

Accent: *London.*

LEGO: Looked as if you could do with a bit of company, know what I mean. I ain't usually wrong. (*Silence.*) Been down here before?

Show you around if you like. Won't cost nothing. Go down the bird park. D'you like birds? (*Silence.*) Last week some kid smashed this bird's legs in with a cricket bat…flamingo…it was in the papers. Know what the RSPCA did? Took it off in a van and put it to sleep. Don't do that to cripples do they. (*Pause.*) So what's the plan for tonight?

Go down the Goose and Duck…lined up like skittles they'll be…scrubbers up one side, bikers down the other…leather boys, you know…creak when they walk. (*He mimes this with sound effects.*) What's hot, hard and throbbing and sticks out between your legs? (*Pause. LEGO mimes revving up a motor bike.*) Vrooom, vroom, vrooom… motor bike. Get it? You should see 'em at closing time… they do wheelies down the waterfront. (*Mimes rearing up*

and riding on the back wheel only.) Vroom, vroooom…
You can rent bikes down here…don't cost much. Ever been
on one? Great ain't they. Rode over a badger once…didn't
half hurt…bit me tongue.

D'you like fun-fairs? There's a great one down here…it's
got a Rota…ever been on one? You know, you go in this
room and stand up against the wall…then the door closes
and the whole place starts going round really fast…then
the friggin' floor disappears…ahhhh… (*He looks at the
floor with all his fingers rammed into his mouth.*) but
you're going so fast you're stuck up against the friggin'
wall like a squashed fly… (*Pulls back his cheeks.*)
G-Force… G-Force…and you've just scoffed a Big Mac,
large french fries smothered in ketchup and a humungous
chocolate milkshake…happened to this kid… threw the
whole lot up… (*With flamboyant finger-wriggling hand
gestures originating from the mouth outwards, he
demonstrates how the kid threw up.*) Blaaaaaa. Looked
like something out *The Exorcist*… (*Pressed up against
the wall in a crucified position. In a deep, demonic
voice.*) I am Beelzebub… (*He makes extravagant
throwing up sounds with illustrative motions*.) You could
see all these kids plastered up against the wall near him
(*Pulling his cheeks back.*) G-Force…G-Force…and this
burgerpuke coming closer and closer… (*He mimes a
tentacle of vomit approaching someone's face…and
then reaching it*.) Ahhhhhhh!

Available in *Yo-Yo*, published by Oberon Books Ltd. Reprinted
by kind permission of the publisher.

ISBN: 1 870259 50 5

FAITH

by Meredith Oakes

Faith was first performed at the Royal Court Theatre Upstairs in October 1997.

The play is set on a small island. A group of soldiers are fighting for possession of the island, but nothing in their training prepares them for the dilemmas they face. Lee Finch is nineteen and a private in the army. His faith is to be ready to die. He, together with his sergeant and other soldiers, have been billeted on the unwilling Sandra, to whom he speaks here. Sandra has just asked him why he has given his sergeant a hard time.

Accent: London.

LEE: He's a sergeant, isn't he. Sergeants are so boring, everyone hates them. Everyone hates them 'cause everyone wants to be mad. And sergeants want to be sane. They want to be sane so badly. They wind up being madder than all the rest of us put together.

No, this is it, they have an impossible task because they have to train us. They have to train us to be hard, see, which means they have to be hard on us. There was one used to get me up five o'clock every morning my first three weeks. Out running before the sun came up, all round the barracks with ice all over the roads and they'd be shouting at us how we were the worst they'd ever had, so weak, no puff, they were all day telling me how thick I was and I'd never make it, it's just, I like to stop and think but you're never supposed to, so they're all the time making out I'm a halfwit because I have thoughts.

They break you right down, they make sure you know exactly how bad life can be when they don't respect you, nothing you do seems to please them and they make you feel like a boil on the face of the earth. Then one day you do something right and someone gives you a good word suggesting they don't hate you quite as much as before. So then the joy of living starts up again, it's like you're born again and they've become your parents, a few weeks down the line and by then you're well in. You're not allowed home the first six weeks. They know what they're doing see. By that time they've become your family, you've won the acceptance and you're really happy they let you belong. Only that's when it comes as a bit of a shock when they let you go off and get killed, because families aren't supposed to be like that.

But this is the sergeant's problem. Because the reason he takes the trouble to be hard on you is that he cares. The more he cares, the more he treats you like a bastard. The more he treats you like a bastard, the more he cares. I don't think it's good for them. They get really strange, some of them. They get really nice to you. It's horrible.

Available in *Faith*, published by Oberon Books Ltd. Reprinted by kind permission of the publisher.

ISBN: 1 870259 80 7

PART TWO: TWENTIES – FEMALE

HENCEFORWARD

by Alan Ayckbourn

Henceforward was first performed at the Stephen Joseph Theatre in the Round, Scarborough in July 1987, and subsequently in London.

The play is set in the future where violence on the streets has escalated to such an extent that certain areas of London have become no-go areas, controlled by marauding girl gangs. Jerome is a reclusive composer, who has hired Zoe – an escort – for personal services. Zoe is an attractive girl in her twenties but has just been attacked by one of the marauding gangs. Her clothes are in ribbons, her face is bleeding from a cut and her hands are torn and filthy. She has lost one shoe and is holding the other. Her stockings are in shreds. She obviously started out looking quite elegant in her smart suit and crisp blouse. This is her first meeting with Jerome.

Accent: English.

ZOE: I'm sorry. (*Brightly.*) Well, here I am. At last. (*She laughs nervously.*) What a super room.

Pause. She nervously indicates a seat.

Is this — for sitting on? Well. Would you mind if I — ? Thanks very much.

She sits. She gives a sudden, quite unexpected, reflex sob as the shock begins to take hold, but elects to continue as if it hadn't happened.

I'm sorry if I'm looking a bit of a – I must do a bit. I'm sorry. Anyway, I understand this was just an initial interview. Mrs Hope-Fitch told me you just wanted to look at me. See if I was suitable. But I believe the actual job's not for a week or so? Have I got that right? (*She sobs.*) Excuse me. Yes?

(*Indicating herself.*) Look, you'll just have to disregard all this. I mean, *this* is ghastly. But I can – you may not believe this – I can look pretty good. Although I say it myself. Yes? But as I say, not – don't, for God's sake, go by this. (*Sobs.*) Sorry.

Would you like me to – walk up and down? Give you an overall picture? People sometimes find it helps them to – get a more general… Of course, I don't quite know what you're looking for so it's a bit… I understand it was slightly unusual? Is that so? (*Sobs.*) I'll stand up. (*She does so.*) There.

Five foot four and a bit. I can lose a bit more weight if you like. I'm a bit over my usual… (*She sobs.*) I'll walk about for you. In case you need me to walk. (*She walks about, limping slightly.*) By the way, I don't usually limp, of course. Please disregard that. I just seem to have bashed my knee — anyway. And, naturally, with heels on I'm that bit taller. They help no end, of course, with all sorts of things. God, look at my legs. Don't look at those, either. I'm sorry, I'm afraid you're just going to have to take my word for an awful lot of things. (*She sobs.*) Look, I'm awfully sorry, I think I'm just going to have to go away somewhere and have a quick cry. I'm sorry, I'm just in a bit of a state. I am sorry. Is there a — ? Have you got a — ? I'll be as quick as I can. I'm so sorry.

Available in *Alan Ayckbourn: Plays One*, published by Faber & Faber Ltd. Reprinted by kind permission of the publisher.

ISBN: 0 571 17680 1

CROSSFIRE

by Michel Azama
(translated by Nigel Gearing)

See note on the play on page 23.

This is a non-naturalistic play about war and war atrocities. It interweaves time, place and generations in a seamless epic and poetic narrative. We know little of the specific backgrounds of any of the characters – often, they are archetypes.

Bella is twenty and a freedom fighter. In this scene she is talking to fifteen-year-old Ismail, her prisoner from the opposing side. War has thrown them together. Bella is tough and cynical beyond her years, accustomed to violence and not afraid of it.

Accent: any.

BELLA: He was called Yossif.

He was more than just a mate. Haven't talked about him for a long time.

When he went off to war I said to myself don't be so melodramatic.

All the women in this country think the same bullshit as you're thinking at this moment…then their men come back.

One day I get a postcard. I'm happy to see his handwriting. But then silence and more silence.

I couldn't imagine him killing anyone. What about you – have you killed anyone?

Right. What was I saying?

I wrote every day no answer. Then one Friday two men in plain clothes at the door. I stuffed my hand into my mouth and bit into it. He'd died February fourth and already been buried two days. I didn't cry. They gave me some water and I looked at the glass shaking in my hand.

It's afterwards it gets tricky. That same evening I asked a friend to take me out. I had to get out. We walked round town. It was curfew. I wanted to say, 'Take me in your arms. Touch me.' I didn't dare. He wouldn't have understood. I don't like you looking at me when I talk about it.

I bumped into one of my girlfriends – we were kids together. It turned out she'd been a war-widow for six years. I wanted to scream. I swore I'd never get like her. I'm not some monument to the dead. I know some who've gone mad. So – then and there – snap out of it, no more moping. My dresses my make-up my jewelry. The pain down here that's nobody's business. Every night I dream I'm dead. It helps.

It's funny. I've always had very simple problems that got complicated the longer I didn't deal with them. Problems with love, of affection, all that stuff. I'd like a good dose of sex to make me forget it all.

Available in *Crossfire*, published by Oberon Books Ltd.
Reprinted by kind permission of the publisher.

ISBN: 1 870259 34 3

KEEPING TOM NICE

by Lucy Gannon

Keeping Tom Nice was first performed by the Royal Shakespeare Company at the Almeida Theatre in August 1988.

Tom is approaching his twenty-fifth birthday. He is severely handicapped and, in spite of the intervention of the social services, has lived in the care of his parents, who have devoted their lives to him. The family is now at breaking point.

Charlie, twenty-three, is Tom's sister. She is at university and lives away from home. She went to university late after working in an office and taking her A levels at night school. She was desperate to make it to university to please her father and 'make up' for Tom. She is bright, apparently loving, but immature. In this scene, she rounds on her mother about the 'neat' way Tom is kept.

Accent: any.

CHARLIE: What is it you're so afraid of, you two? You are, aren't you? You're afraid of something.

Are you afraid that someone will be able to look after Tom as well as you do? Or better? Is that it? It is, isn't it? You want to be the only ones. The holy ones. Dedicated angels. Don't you? You make me sick.

You smooth the bed. You hang flowered wallpaper in his room, you feed him mush when the doctor told you years ago to let him *chew*.

I'm angry because you leave him in here while you watch the TV in there — because all he ever gets at Christmas is

a pair of socks. One year a towel. A towel! All wrapped
up in Santa Claus paper. But most of all I'm angry because
you never, ever kiss him! I have never seen you kiss him.
Hold him. In all the years – never! Oh, not now so much,
not when he's a grown man, but then. I remember kissing
him. How I used to sneak into his room and slide into bed
with him, and whisper to him, silly jokes and childish stories
– we grew up together but I got all the kisses and he got,
what? Soapy flannels? Passive exercises.

He needed those things but not only. Not only! (*Softer.*)
Oh, how could you *not* kiss him? His soft, sleeping body.
His long, thin limbs. The curve of his eyelashes against his
bed-warmed cheeks. For Christ's sake, Mum, whatever
happened to him it happened inside you. That should draw
you together, shouldn't it? He looks at you as if you were a
God. A shining, breathtaking God. You know he does, don't
you?

Available in *Keeping Tom Nice*, published by Warner/
Chappell Plays Ltd. © 1988, 1990 by Lucy Gannon. Reprinted
by kind permission of Warner/Chappell Plays Ltd, London. All
rights reserved. Applications for amateur performance rights
should be addressed to Warner/Chappell Plays Ltd.

ISBN: 0 85676 146 X

SHAKERS: RE-STIRRED

by John Godber and Jane Thornton

Shakers: Re-Stirred was first produced by the Hull Truck Theatre Company in 1991. It is a revised version of a 1984 play, Shakers.

The play is set in Shakers, a glitzy, trendy cocktail bar with pretensions to class in a city centre, somewhere in the UK. The cast of four actresses each play cocktail waitresses, and also role-play various customers. The style is broad and up-front comedy for much of the play, but every so often each of the waitresses steps forward to share her deeper feelings with the audience. Carol is one such waitress, in her twenties.

Accent: any.

CAROL: I can't help it, I hate it when people just assume that because you do a job like this, you're thick. You know there's some nights I just can't stand it. I can't. I want to stand up on top of the bar and shout: I've got O levels, I've got A levels and a Bachelor of Arts Degree. So don't condescend to me, don't pretend you feel sorry for me and don't treat me like I can't read or talk or join in any of your conversations because I can. I see these teenage-like men and women with their well-cut suits and metal briefcases, discussing the City and the arts and time-shares in Tuscany, and I'm jealous, because I can't work out how they've achieved that success. It's so difficult. You see, I want to be a photographer, take portraits. I won a competition in a magazine. It was this photo of a punk sat in a field on an old discarded toilet. It was brilliant. Anyway, after college I had this wonderful idea that I'd go to London with my portfolio. I was confident that I'd get loads of work. But it wasn't like that. The pictures were great, they said, but sorry, no vacancies. My mum said I was being too idealistic wanting it all straight away. My dad said I should settle for a job with the local newspaper, snapping Miss Gazette opening a shoe shop. No thanks. Now he thinks I'm wasting my degree. I was the first in the family to get one so it's not gone down very well. My head's in the clouds, he said, life's not that easy. But it is for some people, like I said, I see them in here. So why should I be different, have they tried harder or something? Maybe they're lucky or it's because they speak nice. It's frustrating because I know how good I am. My dad's right, you know, in some ways: I'm stuck here, wasting away. I do it for the money, that's all. But it won't be forever, no chance. I'm applying for assisting jobs, and as soon as I get one, don't worry, I'm off. I'm now on plan two: start at the bottom and work up. It might take me years, I know that, but it's what keeps me going between the lager and the leftovers. The fact that I know I'll make it in the end.

Available in *Shakers: Re-stirred*, published by Warner/ Chappell Plays Ltd. © 1987, 1993 by John Godber and Jane Thornton. Reprinted by kind permission of Warner/Chappell Plays Ltd, London. All rights reserved. Applications for amateur performance rights should be addressed to Warner/ Chappell Plays Ltd.

ISBN: 0 85676 166 4

AMY'S VIEW

by David Hare

Amy's View was first produced at the Royal National Theatre in June 1997.

The play concerns the troubled mother-daughter relationship between Esmé, an actress, and Amy, her daughter, over a twenty-year period. In this scene, set in 1979, Amy is just twenty-three and has found herself to be pregnant by her boyfriend, Dominic. She is described as 'dark haired, in jeans and a T-shirt, she is thin, with an unmistakeable air of quiet resolution'. Amy is speaking to her mother.

Accent: middle-class English.

AMY: The truth is…my relationship with Dominic has been pretty fragile. It's volatile, is that the word? He can be bad-tempered. He suffers from depression quite badly. At times he…well, he's like…he's a victim of moods.

So the point is, I thought, this is really tricky. Do I just go to him and tell him outright? No, that's going to shock him. And also… I know for a fact he will say to me, look, will I get rid of it? And, for me, there's no question of that. So, alright. It's like solving a puzzle. I want to keep the baby and I want to keep Dominic as well. So I must work out a way of telling him so he doesn't feel pressured, so he doesn't feel, 'oh God, this is just what I feared…'

He said…he has said from the start he wasn't ready for children. He said this. From the very first day. The point is, I made him a promise. No children. He said: 'Whatever else, I can't face starting a family…' (*She stops a moment.*) So you must see that does make things difficult now… Because I just know – I can feel in my stomach – it's going to seem like it's blackmail. For him it'll be like I'm springing a trap. (*She suddenly raises her voice.*) It's everything he feared! I know him. You don't. I tell him now and at once he's going to feel cornered…and when Dominic feels cornered, I tell you, I've seen him, he turns just incredibly stubborn and ugly…

Mother, I'm sorry, but I'm very clear about this. (*She is reluctant, not wanting to go on.*) The fact is…you know… I'd not wanted to tell you…the girl who was with him before… the point is she also…she also got pregnant.

Oh look, I mean it's not…it wasn't immediate. It wasn't like, 'She's pregnant, I'm off…' But it's true. He stopped her having the baby. Then he told me things did start to sour between them. And, pretty soon after, he felt that he'd had enough.

I know… I know, Mother. I know what you're going to say. But the answer is: yes. He is the right man for me. I know this. I know it profoundly. In a way which is way beyond anything.

So it's just a question of what I do now.

Available in *Amy's View*, published by Faber & Faber Ltd. Reprinted by kind permission of the publisher.

ISBN: 0 571 19179 7

THE WOMAN WHO COOKED HER HUSBAND

by Debbie Isitt

The Woman Who Cooked Her Husband was first performed by the Snarling Beasties Company at the University of Warwick in 1991 and subsequently transferred to the Royal Court Theatre in London in October 1991.

Laura is Kenneth's second wife and the biggest problem in their marriage is that she cannot cook as well as his first wife, Hilary. It has awoken other feelings of inadequacy in Laura. Laura is speaking to the audience.

Accent: any.

LAURA: I really didn't know I was capable of such thoughts, it's terrible really – the way they creep up on you when you least expect them – murderous thoughts, cheap and nasty. If only Hilary would disappear – Ken couldn't find so much fault with me – no Hilary to compare me with. If only Hilary wasn't here – Ken would have to eat my meals – without Hilary we could be happy – it's just with her still – around – it makes that hard – a constant reminder of how good things were, how clean things were – how well cooked things were – how well ironed – how neat and how tidy – how I wish that Hilary would have an accident – nothing really horrible like a car crash but maybe roll under something like a bus – instantly squashed – feeling no pain – like a rabbit on a road at night – splat – all over – non-existence – snap my fingers – gone – not there – 'Where's Hilary, I wonder. I popped round to see her and the place was deserted. Perhaps she's run off with a business tycoon' – that would serve him right – but I can't see it

happening overnight. I know it's wrong – God help me, I
know — I just can't help thinking how much easier I'd
feel. No shadowy woman lurking in the past ready to
pounce on me at any minute and tell me what I've done to
her and how happy she made Ken.

I must stop this soon, it leaves a nasty taste in your mouth
– I mean, what's she ever done to me? I never thought I'd
be like this over a man. I've always thought of myself as
independent and free. It shouldn't matter what he thinks –
I shouldn't let him rule my days – I'm sorry God for what I
said about Hilary – she deserves a break – it's just that I
don't think I can cope with life – being such a useless
wife.

ISBN: 0 85676 163 X

A PRAYER FOR WINGS

by Sean Mathias

A Prayer for Wings was first performed at the Edinburgh Festival in August 1985 and was subsequently seen at the Bush Theatre in London.

The play is set in Swansea, South Wales. An old church has been poorly converted into a dwelling. Rita, a plain girl of twenty, lives here in poverty with her sick mam, who suffers from multiple sclerosis and with whom Rita has a complicated relationship. She longs to get away. Mam has just gone to sleep, and Rita addresses the audience.

Accent: South Wales.

RITA: Now I could do it. Do her in. Finish her off. I'd take that pillow and hold it over her head. She's got no strength in that small body of hers. Hardly any fight in them arms. The struggle wouldn't even be noticeable…except…I suppose if they examined her insides, her lungs would be all funny. I suppose it wouldn't look like she'd just passed on in her slumbers. Still, I could run away. Go to a really big city. Go to a really big country. Meet a man. A real man. We'd go out dancing. Go to the cinema. Posh restaurants. And he wouldn't try to interfere. He'd be a real gent. He'd pop the question. On bended knee. I'd say 'Yes. Yes, Boy, I'll have you, to have and to hold, in sickness – God save us – and in health, to our dying day. I'll cook and I'll wash. We'll have our own machine. And I'll give you babies, four boys, lovely little boys. And they'll grow up to be captains. Captains of their teams. Captains of their generations. And we'll be old and comfortable and proud of our boys. Our four boys.' And there'll be no smelly grandparents to have to answer to.

(*To MAM.*) Mam? Are you asleep? Sleeping, Mam?

There's a bad smell in here. A definite bad smell.
I think Mam's started farting. Call this life?

Mam! Settle down, love. I can hear your shuffling.

(*With growing intensity.*) Wishing and wishing and wishing
and wishing and wishing and wishing and wishing and
wishing!

Available in *A Prayer For Wings*, published by Amber Lane
Press. Reprinted by kind permission of the publisher.

ISBN: 0 906399 77 7

THE NEIGHBOUR

by Meredith Oakes

The Neighbour was first produced at the Royal National Theatre in April 1993 as part of the Springboards Festival.

The play is set on a London council estate in the 1990s. Liz shares a flat with her brother, James, and his partner, Stephi. She is unemployed and tends to stay close to home. In this scene, set in the flat, she is speaking to Stephi about her pet mice, Eddy and Freddy. Liz has just made them a woollen pom-pom for their cage.

Accent: London.

LIZ: Look what I made for Eddy and Freddy. (*She holds up the pom-pom.*) Do you want to see me give it them? (*Goes to the cage of Eddy and Freddy.*) Hullo Freddy darling, you in your wheel are you? Oh, the little love, he's a little muscle mouse. Where's your friend? Where's Eddy? Look at him, you can see his little mind going round. Eddy? Eddy? Come and see what Liz has got. Something nice and soft for you. (*To STEPHI.*) Who was that in the car with him? Was that Celestine, was it? (*To mice.*) Oh yes, ain't you a strong little mouse, you can spin that great big wheel all by yourself. Mind you don't catch your tail, that's what happens to little boys who show off. Eddy! I don't know why Eddy won't come out. (*To STEPHI.*) You won't see James till morning then.

He's a law unto himself though, ain't he, you'll never change him. I could never change him. I never had the slightest control. He was such a lovely-looking little boy though. (*To mice.*) Oh yes Freddy, you're a lovely-looking little boy too, you've got a lovely pink nose and it's ever so pointy. Go and get Eddy for me. Go on. (*To STEPHI.*) I hope Eddy's alright. He might be sick, mightn't he. I ought to take off their roof and see what he's up to.

LIZ takes the roof off the cage.

Look at you, you sleepyhead. Don't you want to see what I got for you? Come on, I thought you was supposed to be nocturnal. Here, what you got there? Show Lizzie. Oh! It's a baby! It's a tiny little baby. Fancy that.

Eddy ain't a little boy, he's a mother.

Did you ever see anything so tiny? It looks like it's made of jelly, don't it, like something from the sweet shop. It's like a jellybaby with hands.

LIZ reaches into the cage.

(*To STEPHI.*) I'm only going to put it next its mother. Eddy won't mind, Eddy's my baby, ain't you darling. (*To mice.*) Where's it gone, Eddy, where's your little baby? Look behind you, stupid thing. She's Edwina now. Oh blimey, look at that, will you? She's eating it. Horrible little creature! Horrible little thing! Eating it! Her own baby!

I shouldn't have touched them, it's against their instincts ain't it. You told me not to touch them. You mustn't disturb them, must you. That's what they say. I got what was coming to me, didn't I? But it's unnatural, ain't it? I shan't give them that pom-pom now. It'll go straight in the bin.

Available in *The Neighbour*, published by Oberon Books Ltd. Reprinted by kind permission of the publisher.

ISBN: 1 870259 31 9

THE EDITING PROCESS

by Meredith Oakes

The Editing Process was first performed at the Royal Court Theatre in October 1994.

Tamara del Fuego, twenty-nine, is a corporate image consultant who has been brought in by a major London publishing house to give the image of their latest acquisition 'a radical reassessment'. She prides herself on being exotic and 'arty'. She is talking to Eleanor, a rather colourless young Sloane Ranger, whose uncle runs the company.

Accent: upper-class English.

TAMARA: Do you want to see your new letterhead? It's gorg. (*ELEANOR looks.*) Go on, tell me you love it, it's a mock-up obviously, the editor's name goes there, we can put that in later to avoid any uncertainty. Isn't it beautiful.

That's exactly what I was aiming for, timeless is the next big thing. What's your game plan, Eleanor? When I was your age I had the next ten years mapped out. Well I still am your age.

Sometimes I think what I do is actually therapy, you know? Helping companies through a crisis of identity? Because there's no such thing as a bad company. We're talking a confused company, with myself as the medium through which this company can be released. The company talks to me and I listen. I help the company to express what was previously perhaps too obvious for anyone to mention. When I encourage a company to create its new corporate image, that's like a rite of passage for that company, it achieves a deeper awareness of what it want to project, and I give it the tools it needs to define itself. So it becomes a sort of celebration, a coming of age or a wedding feast, where money should be no object. Should it.

Anyway Lionel told this company I'd be mega. They're not expecting the Seven Wise Virgins. Hostess to a concept is what I am. Well of course the company's given me a budget and I've totally overspent it, and I think everyone should feel they've had a wonderful blow-out and that it's a really special time. I mean I hope your uncle will understand. Perhaps you could have a talk with him. If you're interested, the girl who does my office is having a baby and I'm going to have to replace her, I didn't realise I was harbouring a breeder, I don't pay much but it isn't about pay, ultimately, is it?

Don't think your uncle's going to do anything for you, the owner only uses him for getting into clubs. Don't stay too long, this company's dodgier than eggs. Yes, I'm transforming its fortunes with a new corporate image. I am. This company's going to die with a smile on its face.

Available in *The Editing Process*, published by Oberon Books Ltd. Reprinted by kind permission of the publisher.

ISBN: 1 870259 46 7

PENTECOST

by Stewart Parker

Pentecost was first performed in the Guildhall, Derry, by the Field Day Theatre Company in September 1987 and was subsequently produced at the Lyric Theatre, Hammersmith.

The play is set in Belfast in 1974. Ruth is twenty-nine and has been married for ten years to a violent husband, David. David is a policeman in the Royal Ulster Constabulary. She has left her husband three times before, but always gone back to him. Now, in the early hours of the morning, she has turned up at the new home of Marian, her childhood friend. Ruth is talking to Marian throughout this speech.

Accent: Belfast.

RUTH: It's quite hard, getting here. That fire's quite warm. I know it's a bit late to be asking, I would have phoned only you haven't got one, I did actually phone, at the flat, and the shop, not knowing, but anyway — if there was any chance, you could maybe put me up for the night. Marian. I have decided, actually. To leave — David.

I'm not making excuses for him. He's not a bad person, Marian, honest to God, his nerves are frayed away to nothing…

They never know the minute, he's had three good mates killed in his own station, and a fourth one blinded, it's the waiting around all day that gets to him, all the threats and the hatred and no outlet, he comes home coiled up like a spring, he's frightened of his life, it's all pent up inside him… Christ, I'm no better, sitting at home, waiting to hear the worst… I caught my sleeve on one of his swimming

trophies – Waterford crystal it was — it smashed to bits in
the hearth… I just stared down, stupid, at the pieces like a
child who knows it's in for a thumping…it was a sort of
blinding crunch and a flash of light. I was lying behind the
sofa then and I could feel my hair getting wet…twice more
he hit me…but I had my arms up by then…the phone
started to ring. I think that saved me, not that he answered
it, it sort of half brought him round, he just stared down at
me and said, 'that's you sorted out', and then he threw the
truncheon into a corner and went into the hall for his coat
and I heard the front door slamming. He hadn't even had
his dinner. So I got up and cleaned myself off — I knew
then I had to go, get away — I didn't want to be there
when he got back, not this time — I really knew this time I
couldn't live with him anymore — how can you love
somebody once you're actually in fear of your life of him
— I don't blame him, Marian, but I can't stay with him, I
can't stand being so scared…
I'm sorry.

Available in *Three Plays For Ireland*, published by Oberon
Books Ltd (out of print). Reprinted by kind permission of
the publisher.

ISBN: 1 870259 17 3

I AM YOURS

by Judith Thompson

I Am Yours was first presented by Tarragon Theatre, Toronto in November 1987 and by Shared Experience at the Royal Court Theatre in February 1998.

Mercy has come to visit her sister, Dee, who she finds is pregnant. Both women are disturbed by their past experiences. In this scene, Mercy has just heard Dee tell the father of her child that she wants nothing to do with him and will give the baby away.

Accent: American or Canadian.

MERCY: That was a hideous thing to do. That was a disgusting, cruel, horrific…

No, no, this time I will not get off your case.

You make me sick you are so smug and beautiful, you have no idea what it is to be me, all the boys looking straight at you, never at me. That time at the dance when you went straight up to Stephen Gilroy who you knew was crazy about you and said, 'Oh dance with Mercy, she loves you so much'. And the other time in front of all our friends when you made me pick my nose and eat it; you said I had to, to get in your club, that you'd all done it. And then I did it. And you laughed, you laughed. Do you know how much I hated you? Do you know how much?

If you're a woman and you're born ugly you might as well be born dead. Don't. Don't you laugh.

Don't put down television, you snot, television has saved my life. It has literally saved my life, when you're so lonely

you could die. I mean shrivel up and die because nobody
cares whether you get up or stay in bed or don't eat, when
you're so lonely every pore in your skin is screaming to be
touched, the television is a saviour. It is a voice, a warm
voice. There are funny talk shows with hosts who think
exactly like I do. And when the silence in your apartment,
the silence is a big nothing and you're thinking, my God, my
God, is this what life is? Years and years and years of this?
You turn on the television and you forget about it. Often all
I'll think about all day at work is what's on TV that night,
especially in the fall, with all the new shows, I get really,
genuinely excited. I… I love television. I love it. It makes
me happy so don't put it down.

Available in *I Am Yours*, published by Faber & Faber Ltd.
Reprinted by kind permission of the publisher.

ISBN: 0 571 19612 8

I AM YOURS

by Judith Thompson

See note on the play on page 53.

Dee is a disturbed young woman, frightened by her own capacity for violence. As a result of this fear she has separated from her husband and now finds herself pregnant by the supervisor of her apartment building. She opts for an abortion. In this scene, Dee has left her pre-surgery bed and wandered down the halls, in her gown. She has felt the life of the foetus inside her and cannot go through with the abortion. She addresses the audience as if it is the foetus.

Accent: American or Canadian.

DEE: A feeling like a push; somebody strong, pushing me off the table, it was not a…decision, I was pushed and I felt and I feel and I hear…a breathing…inside me, that is not my own. I do…hear it. A raspy kind of sweet breathing a – a – pulling for breath, for air and kind of a sigh of content. I feel the breath on my face the drops of wet breath, hear a sigh, are you there? A voice not mine, a voice like no other; there you are, in the sighing, and I know I think I know whose voice this is; this is yours, this is yours, this is not a mirage, no, not part of the madness, a moment of clear, oh yes, you are clear, I can taste your sweet breath, a flower, not mine, not mine but inside me I can feel on my hand the press of your hand, fingers, holding my hand, tiny fingernails, not letting go, the impression, the feel of a tiny body lying next to mine, breathing, in the bed, cream sheets.
I am asleep; how can I see this? How? You are showing me, showing me, you are looking at me with your dark blue

eyes, staring at me in the dark in the night, smelling my
milk, breathing fast for my milk, the shininess of your eyes
like the moon on the water I see: I see it, in my mind, too
clearly, just as I can hear your voice, too too clear, rising,
falling, your eyes, looking at me from across the room,
watching me move across the kitchen, watching me; when
I hold you and you wrap your hair around your tiny hands,
pulling, and your head on my chest rooting for the breast, I
can hear, I can feel the rooting. I am lost, I have heard you,
I can feel you drinking of me, you drink my milk and you
drink and you drink and, oh, I am lost.

Available in *I Am Yours*, published by Faber & Faber Ltd.
Reprinted by kind permission of the publisher.

ISBN: 0 571 19612 8

PART TWO: TWENTIES – MALE

SUGAR SUGAR

by Simon Bent

Sugar Sugar was first performed at the Bush Theatre in July 1998.

The play is set in a guesthouse in Scarborough, in winter. The guesthouse is run by Val who was 'a bit of a goer' in her youth. Her family, like her establishment, is in disrepair. Then an enigmatic visitor arrives – Dennis Wilson – and brings a sexual charge that electrifies the household and threatens to tip it over the edge. In this scene he is talking to Val, who is upset because of her son's deteriorating marriage. Here, Dennis is consciously identifying with her inner feelings, making himself ever more sympathetic. The delivery is almost hypnotic as he works his unusual seduction technique.

Accent: any.

DENNIS: You need a cup of tea. I've put the kettle on.

He pours a large glass of dandelion and burdock and drinks it in one.

I know that something good or bad is happening, that it's about to happen and that I'm not where I should be…I forget everything – years, people, days…gone, dissolved… trembling – the walls close in…my heart trembles – I sit, I smoke, I stand, walking with fear, shaking, every breath is my last – each cigarette lasts a lifetime, an eternity to smoke – I don't smoke – I get the fear, I get the fear and there's nothing – it's all nothing and I cling on for the light, if it's still the same, if it hasn't gone – in the morning, in the cold clear light of day…dissolving – every day and I feel like a foreigner…I can't remember.

It's alright when I'm lying down. I lie awake at night with my eyes open…a loving mother, a loving father, a loving woman to wrap their arms around me…in the end I wrap my arms around myself…and I start praying …'Oh dear Lord'… 'Please dear Lord' – and I can't get up and I think everything would be alright if only I was dead and I don't want to die and then I get up. I can't think of anyone.

You're not stupid.

No, you're not.

I bet you were a very attractive young girl. A very very attractive girl.

Tell me you're a very attractive woman. Say it.

Of course you can. A very attractive woman.

That's right.

Available in *Sugar Sugar*, published by Oberon Books Ltd. Reprinted by kind permission of the publisher.

ISBN: 1 84002 033 4

THE DARKER FACE OF THE EARTH

by Rita Dove

The Darker Face of the Earth, by the USA's former poet laureate, was first performed at the Oregon Shakespeare Festival in July 1996 and in the UK at the Royal National Theatre in August 1999.

The play is set in South Carolina, in the Southern United States, in the 1840s. The action takes place on the Jennings Plantation. Twenty years previously, Amalia Jennings gave birth to a son by a black slave. The child was smuggled out of the plantation. Now the charismatic slave Augustus, of mixed parentage, has come to the plantation. Augustus is a tall, handsome young man with caramel-toned skin and piercing eyes, his righteous anger thinly concealed behind his slave mannerisms. He is speaking to Amalia, with whom he has a challenging relationship.

Accent: Southern American.

AUGUSTUS: Now I have a story for you.
  Once there was a preacher slave
  went by the name of Isaac.
  When God called him
  he was a boy, out hunting ricebirds.
  Killing ricebirds is easy –
  just pinch off their heads.

Indicating the sherry.

May I?

AMALIA flinches, nods. He pours the sherry expertly.

But one day, halfway up the tree
where a nest of babies chirped,
a voice called out: 'Don't do it, Isaac.'
It was an angel, shining
in the crook of the branch.
Massa let him preach.
What harm could it do.

Sitting down in the damask chair.

Then a slave uprising in Virginia
had all the white folks
watching their own niggers
for signs of treachery.
No more prayer meetings, Isaac!
But God would not wait,
so Isaac kept on preaching
at night, in the woods.

Of course, he was caught.
Three of his congregation
were shot on the spot, three others branded
and their feet pierced.
But what to do about Isaac,
gentle Isaac who had turned traitor.

First they flogged him. Then
they pickled the wounds with salt water,
and when they were nearly healed,
he was flogged again, and the wounds
pickled again, and on and on for weeks
while Massa sold off Isaac's children
one by one. They took him to see
his wife on the auction block,
baby at her breast.
A week later it was his turn.
His back had finally healed;
but as his new owner led him
from the auction block,
Isaac dropped down dead.

Pause; more to himself than AMALIA.

They couldn't break his spirit,
so they broke his heart.

Available in *The Darker Face of the Earth*, published by
Oberon Books Ltd. Reprinted by kind permission of the publisher.

ISBN: 1 84002 129 2

WITTGENSTEIN'S DAUGHTER

by Dic Edwards

Wittgenstein's Daughter was first performed at the Citizens Theatre, Glasgow in September 1998.

The play is a serious comedy concerning Alma Wittgenstein, daughter of the influential philosopher. Bored by her neo-fascist husband and the threat he poses to her values, she goes to Cambridge to investigate the ideas of her late father. Here she meets one of her father's old friends, the one hundred-year-old ex-boxer, Beckett. Here, Beckett appears as he was when he first met Wittgenstein, as twenty-one-year-old Young Beckett, a boxer. He talks to the audience.

Accent: *Cockney.*

YOUNG BECKETT: I like telling the troof. I'm an 'omosexual. Me. Terry Beckett. Boxer. Age twenty-one. I don't mind 'oo knows. Warr annoys me is, I come to these parties regular. I get into 'em cos I'm an 'omosexual. Only tonight, the bloke at the door didn' wannit. Didn' wanttu let me in. So he puts on that voice: you know: I'm fwightfully sowwy. Meaning: you can't fuckin' come in. And you will find up and down this land that speaking like that counts. But iss like a game. Just keeps you duckin' and divin' all ovu the place. Iss part of their weapons, those words like jewels in the 'andle of a ceremonial dagger. And you can't get past their words in frough the door. (*He hits something.*) You see 'em in their bit of town round King's Parade all the toffs, the students. That's why they call it that cos they're all aparading like kings but the townies don't like 'em and you can't blame 'em, they was 'ere

first, the townies. Iss like the townies are just there tu
serve the toffs. Get 'em into our bit of town and you can
serve 'em wiv an uppercut. (*Uppercuts*.) So I says: I
know you can stop me comin' in because wiv that voice
you got the auffowity. *But* can you wiv that voice tell the
trooff? Can you wiv that voice say: I am an 'omosexual?
And I know that 'e is 'cos it's an 'omosexual's party and
'e's on the fuckin' door! So I says: I can. I can say it. I am
an 'omosexual! Wiv that they let me in! Then I meet this
bloke quite quickly and we come up to this room and 'e
shuts the door and immediately 'ides down by the side of
the bed!

Available in *Wittgenstein's Daughter*, published by Oberon
Books Ltd. Reprinted by kind permission of the publisher.

ISBN: 1 870259 35 1

SUSAN'S BREASTS

by Jonathan Gems

Susan's Breasts was first performed by the English Stage Company at the Royal Court Theatre Upstairs in May 1985.

The play concerns the difficulties of love among a group of successful twenty-somethings. Lemon is twenty-four, good-looking and muscular with long hair. He has rich parents and is decidedly eccentric in both dress and manner. He is talking to Susan, with whom he is obsessively in love. Previously he has kidnapped her and as a result has been committed to a psychiatric hospital by his parents. Susan is an actress. A doctor told her she was sterile but she now finds herself pregnant.

Accent: *any.*

LEMON: I love you. Let's get married. Course I'd have to get out of Whitecroft first. I need you to help me do that. And then, as soon as I'm declared sane we'll have lots of money…'cause it was my twenty-fifth birthday recently, so I've got my grandfather's money to pick up. The inheritance. But I have to be sane to get the money. It's in the terms of the trust. And then we could hit the road. Travel. Go anywhere. Have the baby in Italy or Venezuela or Connecticut. Get away from all these nazis everywhere.

It'll be great! What's the matter? All we do is, first, get me out of that dump, then… Look, would you mind if we don't get married in a church? I hate churches. What I'd really like is to get married in the woods. There's a place near where my granny lives. Near Bournemouth. Primrose Wood. It's a completely magical place. There are actually fairies there. I've seen them.

What's the matter? Are you alright?

Oh well, we don't have to get married. It's stupid marriage anyway, isn't it? We love each other, that's what matters. And we're going to have a baby. It's a miracle. So, I'd better start behaving myself. The trouble is I'm in there with a whole lot of complete loonies. It's a bad atmosphere. And they keep giving me drugs. I'm caught in a trap.

My parents had to get me certified. They had to. It was either that or go to prison. I've behaved incredibly badly towards them. Especially my father. I don't know why because really the only evil thing they ever did to me was to send me to public school. But, Susan, if we could get married and leave the country, we could be so happy. You and me together. Start afresh.

SUSAN begins to shrink away from him.

I think about you all the time. I dream about being with you in the desert, in the jungle, in the mountains – all sorts of places. I dream about getting a house with you. I can see it. Like the Dulux commercial. Lots of bright sunshine and white paint. And filling you up with babies and surrounded by dogs and cats and birds and hens pecking in the yard. Domesticity! Accomplishments! Making a hen-house. Putting new spark plugs in the car. Scraping the carrots, earning a living. Whatever we have to do.

Available in *Jonathan Gems: Three Plays*, published by Oberon Books Ltd. Reprinted by kind permission of the publisher.

ISBN: 1 870259 10 6

PLAYING SINATRA

by Bernard Kops

Playing Sinatra was first performed at the Warehouse Theatre, Croydon in October 1991.

The play concerns an obsessive, exclusive brother-sister relationship between Norman and Sandra. Norman is an agoraphobic bookbinder who is obsessed with the life and music of Frank Sinatra. Their lives are changed when Phillip de Groot enters Sandra's life and threatens to tear Norman and Sandra apart. Philip is a charming, good-looking, open man who smiles a lot. His voice is soft and gentle. He always listens and never interrupts.

Accent: *any.*

PHILLIP: I am a seeker. I used to be an architect. Not bad. Mainly hack work; the exigencies of modern life. The realities. The compromises one has to make. Then one day, whilst walking in China. I was walking along the Great Wall actually, when I had a kind of mystical experience. It was if you like my Road to Damascus. An inner voice boomed. Phillip de Groot! What are you doing with your life? What was I doing indeed? From that moment on I was plagued with inner doubt. What is the meaning of me? What is the meaning of existence? Is there a meaning? Should there be a meaning? *Qui somme-nous*? *Ou allons-nous.* The binding is the person, indeed. But my binding fell away. I was terrified. I almost fell apart.

Sandra gives him a biscuit.

Ginger snaps. How very nice. How did you know these were my favourites? Anyway, I survived that greatest crisis in my life. And I chucked it all in. I dabbled in many things, trying to find my new self. I've travelled extensively in India. Did voluntary work among the bereft of Africa. All the time questioning, surviving. You see me as I am, a seeker. I believe we are the stuff that dreams are made of but we, man, humankind, is in terrible danger. And we are the danger. I have a modest income. A legacy. I am content, yet not complacent. I am still searching for my true vocation. I hope that answers your question.

Available in *Bernard Kops: Plays One*, published by Oberon Books Ltd. Reprinted by kind permission of the publisher.

ISBN: 1 84002 071 7

THE COLOUR OF JUSTICE

edited by Richard Norton-Taylor

The Colour of Justice was first performed at the Tricycle Theatre, Kilburn in January 1999 and subsequently on TV and at the Royal National Theatre.

The play is based on the harrowing transcripts of the Stephen Lawrence public enquiry. In 1993 black teenager Stephen Lawrence was stabbed to death in a racist attack by a gang of white youths. The police investigation failed to produce sufficient evidence to convict. Here, Duwayne Brooks, a young black Londoner and contemporary of Stephen, now in his early twenties, tells of the night of the murder and his experience afterwards.

Accent: Black South London.

DUWAYNE: On the eighth of May, I went to a large anti-racist demonstration outside the British National Party headquarters in Welling. I went to protest against Steve's murder and the way the police were handling it. In October 1993, I was arrested and charged with offences arising out of the demonstration. They waited until the Crown Prosecution Service had decided to drop the prosecution against the killers. It was devastating. It felt like the police and prosecutors decided to get at me to ruin my reputation – and the chance to get any future prosecution for the murders. But the judge at Croydon Crown Court wasn't having any of it. In December 1994, he stopped the prosecution saying it was an abuse of the process of the court.

I think of Steve every day. I'm sad, confused and pissed about this system where racists attack and go free but innocent victims like Steve and I are treated as criminals and at the outset ignored me when I pointed out where the killers had run and refused to believe me that it was a racist attack.

I never knew Steve to fight no-one. Steve wasn't used to the outside world. He wasn't street-aware of the dangers of being in a racist area at night-time. I shouted to run. He had ample time to run as the boys were on the other side of the road. Steve didn't understand that the group of white boys was dangerous.

I was taken to the identification parade. I saw a skinhead there, Stacey Benefield. He said the boys who stabbed him were known to stab people and not to get done for it. He said they knew people in the police. I now know that the person I picked out was Neil Acourt.

On the third identification parade, I now know I identified Luke Knight. Sergeant Crowley said something to the effect that I was guessing. I got angry. I recognised the attackers from the attack and not from any outside information. Nobody described the Acourt brothers to me. I did not know how important Sergeant Crowley's lies were until I heard it on the news that the two men who had been arrested had been released and it was to do with my evidence not being good enough.

Available in *The Colour of Justice*, published by Oberon Books Ltd. Reprinted by kind permission of the publisher.

ISBN: 1 84002 107 1

THE NEIGHBOUR

by Meredith Oakes

See note on the play on page 47.

The play is set on a London council estate where two young men, John and James, who live next door to each other, suddenly become enemies, invoking destructive forces beyond their control. The community takes sides like spectators cheering from a grandstand as the conflict escalates into tragedy. Here James is talking to Stephi, the young woman with whom he lives, and his sister, Liz.

Accent: London.

JAMES: You're far more interested in me than I am in you. But then, what's there to know about you? Do you think I feel jealous? I don't. That's how predictable you are. I see you with someone else, it don't bother me.

Next time you're talking to your friend next door, remember to thank him for destroying my credibility. I'm skint, ain't I. I'm unemployed. I'm going to have to live off you from now on, and you can't even afford to keep me in this hairstyle. What you being so quiet for? Tired are you. You ought to get a better job. Since you been out cleaning your hands are like alligator paws. They ain't soft like they used to be.

This ain't the first time that things have gone wrong for me. But I'm lucky. My enemies go down and I survive. You want to know what I'm capable of. I'm capable of anything. What you want me to do? You want a demonstration. What you doing with the kettle, Liz? Give it here. Come on, give it, it ain't yours. Now watch this, Steph. I'm going to throw it on you, look.

Makes as if to throw it. LIZ screams.

Don't you trust me? What you take me for? You got
a high opinion of me, ain't you. I can't make you out.
You're living every day with someone who puts you in
fear. It's unbalanced.

Available in *The Neighbour*, published by Oberon Books Ltd.
Reprinted by kind permission of the publisher.

ISBN: 1 870259 31 9

FAITH

by Meredith Oakes

See note on the play on page 29.

Private Mick Pike is a soldier, aged twenty, stationed on an island somewhere in the South Atlantic during a time of war. He is talking to his comrade in arms, Lee.

Accent: any.

MICK: The way I look at it. An order which is so obviously questionable has to be, by definition, an order that was made with very good reason. It's not as if they like making questionable orders. So obviously if he finds he has to make an order like that, such an obviously questionable order, the last thing he wants is for anyone to question it.

The problem with something like this. A questionable order like this. We assume it results out of careful deliberation. We assume there are special circumstances. We assume that all the careful deliberation which people have been doing for years has finally resulted in someone having the right to make this questionable order in special circumstances.

Of course all the time it might just have come from some twat.

I haven't thought about anything back home since we got here. How many people back home have ever been tested. How many of them would be ready to die for their faith. What's your faith Lee.

Being ready to die? Is that it.

I'm not really ready to die.

Why should I die for them. All they want is a chance to get on with their selfish little imaginary little lives.
I'd die for my mates. Because we've earned it. As for the rest of them. Living on in their kingdom of light with their cities and their glorious pavements and their freedom parades, walking on the dust that used to be us, well they're laughing aren't they. I hate them. Maybe it's not even worth hanging around if I just have to be with them.

Available in *Faith*, published by Oberon Books Ltd. Reprinted by kind permission of the publisher.

ISBN: 1 870259 80 7

PART THREE: THIRTIES – FEMALE

MAN OF THE MOMENT

by Alan Ayckbourn

Man of the Moment was first performed at the Globe Theatre, London in February 1990.

The play is set on the paved pool/patio area of a modern, moderately sized villa in a Spanish-speaking area of the Mediterranean, owned by former criminal and now TV personality, Vic Parks. Jill Rillington, in her early thirties and looking good – certainly at first glance – is every inch the assured, charming TV reporter/presenter. This is the opening moment of the play. She is doing a piece to camera, though, Ayckbourn comments, we won't guess this immediately.

Accent: any.

JILL: (*To camera.*) Hallo. I'm Jill Rillington. In this edition of *Their Paths Crossed*, we tell a story that started seventeen years ago in the slow and sneet of a Surrey Novem... Oh, piss! Keep rolling. We'll go again. Snow and sleet. Snow and sleet... (*Slowly.*) Snow – and – sleet... Here we go. Snow and sleet. Hallo. I'm Jill Rillington. In this edition of *Their Paths Crossed*, we tell a story that started seventeen years ago in the snow and sleet of a Surrey November morning, and finishes – (*She gestures.*) here. In the brilliant sunshine of a glorious Mediterranean summer. It's a story which has – fittingly perhaps – almost a fairy tale ring to it. A tale with a hero and a villain – even a damsel in distress. But this is no child's fable, it is a true story. This is the real world where nothing is as it seems. This is the real world where heroes are easily forgotten; this is the real world where the villains may, themselves, become heroes. And as for distressed damsels – well, are they in reality ever truly rescued? I'll leave you, the viewer, to judge for yourself…

She pauses for a moment, looking towards the camera.

And – cut! OK? Did you get the wide? (*Gesturing.*) The wide?

Good. Did you get this whole area? (*Gesturing and yelling.*) This whole area?

What? (*She notices her radio mic.*) Oh, yes. Sorry, Dan. Didn't mean to burst your eardrums. Sorry, my love. (*She consults her watch. She makes to yell again then thinks better of it.*) George – (*Quietly.*) Sorry, love. Dan, can you tell George to set up the arrival shot. For the arrival. Can he do that? Where we talked about? On the bend? So we see this man's taxi coming up the hill and their first meeting at the front door? OK? George knows where. I'll be with you in a sec. Thank you, love. I'll unplug. Save your batteries.

Available in *Alan Ayckbourn: Plays One*, published by Faber & Faber Ltd. Reprinted by kind permission of the publisher.

ISBN: 0 571 17680 1

THE MAI

by Marina Carr

The Mai was first produced at the Peacock Theatre, Dublin in October 1994.

This is a memory play. Thirty-year-old Millie looks back on her sixteen-year-old self and her family at their house on the shores of Owl Lake, in the Irish Republic. The 'Mai' of the title is Millie's own mother, Mai, who at times seems almost like a creature from mythology. In an effort to escape her mother's emotional clutches, Millie has turned her back on home and family. Now, with the Mai dead, she has returned to the house by Owl Lake to confront her ghosts.

Accent: Irish.

MILLIE: Joseph, my five-year-old son, has never been to Owl Lake. I thought of having him adopted but would not part with him when the time came, and I'm glad, though I know it's hard for him. Already he is watchful and expects far too little of me, something I must have taught him unknown to myself. He is beginning to get curious about his father and I don't know what to tell him. I tell him all the good things. I say your Daddy is an El Salvadorian drummer who swept me off my feet when I was lost in New York. I tell him his eyes are brown and his hair is black and that he loved to drink Jack Daniels by the neck. I tell him that high on hash or marijuana or god-knows-what we danced on the roof of a tenement building in Brooklyn to one of Robert's cello recordings.

I do not tell him that he is married with two sons to a jaded uptown society girl or that I tricked him into conceiving you because I thought it possible to have something for myself that didn't stink of Owl Lake. I did not tell him that on the day you were born, this jaded society queen sauntered into the hospital, chucked you under the chin, told me I was your Daddy's last walk on the wild side, gave me a cheque for five thousand dollars and said, you're on your own now, kiddo. And she was right. I had no business streelin' into her life, however tired it was. I do not tell him that, when you were two, I wrote a sensible letter, enclosing a photograph of you, asking him to acknowledge paternity. And I do not tell you he didn't answer.

Available in *The Mai*, published by The Gallery Press. Reprinted by kind permission of the author and The Gallery Press.

ISBN: 1 85235 161 6

SILLY COW

by Ben Elton

Silly Cow was first performed at the Theatre Royal, Haymarket in February 1991.

This comedy centres on the repellent Doris Wallis, queen of the tabloid press who is, in her own words, 'a nasty cow who slaughters sacred cows'. Described by the author as 'bitchy, brassy and bolshie' she is every inch as unpleasant as the public persona she so carefully cultivates. In this scene Doris is due to be interviewed on 'Wogan', a TV chat show. She is speaking to Sidney, a tabloid newspaper man who 'likes to think of himself as a rough diamond' and who has been trying to persuade Doris to sign a contract with him.

Accent: any.

DORIS: Well, pardon me if I don't chew your trousers off and kiss the great man's bum. I've said I'll probably take the job and I really don't see why I should have to sign anything.

I just have a problem with signing things, that's all. I think I must have been scared by a contract as a small child.

Of course I trust you, Candyfloss. I trust all editors to be dirty, duplicitous little weasels and not one has ever failed me. You're not the only one who'll be giving things up, Sidney Skinner! You're not the only one who's had to work hard for everything they've got. While you were sneaking around Hollywood trying to buy photos of Jackie Onassis with her fun bags flying, I was dogsbody on the *Preston Clarion*, and I mean dogsbody.

Yes, and I'm never going back. These last few years I've finally got a grip of *la dolce vita* and I'm sticking my talons in deep. I am never again going to get up at five-thirty on a rainy morning to report on a sheepdog trial, I am never again going to cover the Liberal candidate in a by-election, and I am never again going to review another show at Preston Rep.

There was this appalling old ham; I'd watched him every three weeks for two-and-a-half years, and whatever part he played, he did his Noël Coward impression. Hamlet's ghost, Noël Coward. *The Crucible*, Noël Coward, *Mother Courage*, Noël Coward. Imagine what the old fart was like when he actually had to play in a Noël Coward – his accent got so clipped I swear he was only using the first letter of each word. So please believe me, Sidney, I am never going back to that. I've done my time, Sidney, and now it's paying off. I've got my own column, I've cooked with Rusty on TV-AM, two *Blankety Blanks* last series, and Les called me Cuddles. What's more, tonight is the big one, I get my first *Wogan*. These are not things you throw away lightly, Sidney. Which is why I am just a little bit hesitant about ending up in Stuttgart working for an editor I scarcely know… I don't like being pushed around and I certainly wouldn't dream of signing anything without showing it to Peggy. If Peggy thinks it necessary, she'll show it to a lawyer. Anyway, it'll have to do. I'm not going to change again.

Available in *Silly Cow*, published by Warner Books. Reprinted by kind permission of the author.

ISBN: 0 7515 0190 5

FAITH

by Meredith Oakes

See note on the play on page 29.

The play is set in a remote island farmhouse at a time of war, 1982. A group of English soldiers are fighting for possession of the island. Nothing in their training prepares them for this situation. They have billeted themselves with Sandra, a farmer's wife in her thirties. She is talking to the soldiers, whose presence she resents, during this scene.

Accent: any regional accent.

SANDRA: The spring here is beautiful. It's beautiful with the sun shining, and the wind blowing the grass all up the hillsides and the quiet in the valleys. The little flowers are amazing… Sea pinks along the headland, daisies, there's actually a daisy that smells like chocolate, they call it the vanilla daisy… The air in this place is normally so clean, you notice the change when you get within a mile of town, you start smelling the petrol, that's how clean the air is normally. Normally you could go round the beaches and see elephant seals. The animals never learned the fear of man. God they must be thick. I have to get the dinner.

Think it's rubbish here don't you. Think we're rubbish. How you can make out you want to fight for us…you want to fight because you want to fight and that's all. And if we're rubbish… What are you? You're dossers. If you weren't doing this. You'd all be on the social. If it wasn't for all this. Where would you be? Living in some flat on some estate, and your biggest thrill of the day would be cutting your toenails with the breadknife. Dregs of society, you are. Get yourselves killed, best thing for everyone. It's such a crying shame. That the opposite sex. Had to be men.

Available in *Faith*, published by Oberon Books Ltd. Reprinted by kind permission of the publisher.

ISBN: 1 870259 80 7

PART THREE: THIRTIES – MALE

TOAST

by Richard Bean

Toast was first performed at the Royal Court Theatre Upstairs in February 1999.

The play is set in 1975 and covers the Sunday night shift in a Yorkshire bread plant. Seven men come together to bake enough bread to feed the population of Hull. Robert Blakey is the chargehand. He wears baker's whites which have seen three or four shifts, and a striped office shirt with an open collar. He wears Buddy Holly black spectacles. His hair is mid-seventies style with sideburns. His sleeves are rolled up. He is a physical man, prone to bouncing on his feet and touching his crotch unnecessarily. He has tattoos on each forearm. He fantasises about being a rock 'n' roll performer. He is showing Lance, a mature student, around the plant – it is Lance's first night at work.

Accent: *Yorkshire.*

BLAKEY: (*Offering his hand.*) Blakey, Robert Blakey. This is Walter Nelson. Our mixer. (*Shakes hands.*) We work a six-day week. Nights is three till finish. Finish can be anywhere between eleven at night to three in't morning. Wednesdays and Thursdays we work a twelve-hour shift – seven at night till seven in't morning. Last day is Friday – three till finish again. That's a sixteen-hour day on Friday and maybe a few hours of Saturday morning thrown in. Then you're back here again Sunday morning at seven. How's that grab yer?

Is it legal? You get paid. Bit old for a student, aren't you? Let me see your hands. I gorra check for dermatitis.

BLAKEY takes LANCE's hands and turns them palms up. He sees LANCE has a scarred left wrist and pushes up LANCE's cuff for a better look at his wound.

If I were you I'd keep them cuffs rolled down like you had 'em. Our oven won't bite so hard that way.

BLAKEY goes to a cupboard and takes out two pairs of coarse sackcloth oven gloves, which he gives to LANCE.

Wear two pair of gloves. Last student we had lasted two hours. I had to tek him to infirmary mesen. Crying he was. Sociologist. Come with me, Sir Lancelot. I'm gonna put you on the oven. You ever seen a reel oven? It's not dangerous so long as you keep up with it, and don't panic when it gets ahead.

The phone rings. BLAKEY answers it.

(*On the phone.*) Bread plant… Yeah, it's me… Hello Mr Beckett, what's up… You wanna come in and do a shift?… Ha, ha! I'd treat yer well… Mmm… Mm… You what?… Are you pulling my plonker?… How many?… That'll tek us till four in the morning. How many again?… Wi' lids?… Right… Well, you could've told 'em to fuck off… Yeah, yeah, yeah, yeah… I know, if Bradford ses bek it we gorra bek it… They'll send an artic yeah?… Right, tarra.

(*He puts the phone down and turns to WALTER.*) Skeltons 'ave 'ad a fuck-up. Bradford are telling us to do three thousand for 'em. Big uns, aye. (*To LANCE.*) Huh, you're gonna 'ave some fun tonight sunshine.

Available in *Toast*, published by Oberon Books Ltd. Reprinted by kind permission of the publisher.

ISBN: 1 84002 104 7

TOAST

by Richard Bean

See note on the play on page 87.

Lance is in his mid-thirties. He wears country tweeds and leather brogues, and a red rugby shirt with a white collar. His hair is collar-length and unkempt. He is a mature student of social and economic history, working his first shift at a Yorkshire bread plant. Here he is speaking to Walter, known as 'Nellie' – a broken man of fifty-nine. Lance is winding Nellie up – or is he?

Accent: *Yorkshire.*

LANCE: Would it be possible to touch you for a cigarette? I normally eschew the weed, on health grounds naturally, but in situations like this the pressure of social conformity is greater than my will to live. I'm using 'will to live' there as a figure of speech naturally – having raged unsuccessfully against the dying of the light several years ago.

I'm not a student Walter. I'm not at school. I'm here to see you. I can't tell you Walter, being dead has made a significant difference to my life. I have no concerns about my health, and I groom less. (*Beat.*) It is very opportune for me – being 'on a smoke' whilst you are taking your half-hour. Alone in the canteen. It is quite perfect. One might even say designed. I feared that I would have to corner you in the lavatory or steal thirty seconds in the mixing room, just to be with you.

Pause.

Are you prepared Walter?

That is exactly what I said! How can one prepare? Death is the only real adventure. Planning, preparation, making ready – all tosh! A willing acquiescence with fate is all that one can reasonably contribute. (*Beat.*) I have told them but they take very little notice of me. I said take him, snatch him away, suddenly. Why go to the expense of sending a messenger? Do you realise, Walter, to send me here has required eight signatures on two separate requisitions. One for the exceptional expenditure incurred, and one for a four-day visa.

Where am I from? The other side. From across the metaphorical water. No Walter, not Grimsby. The land of living souls and rotting bodies. The next world. I'm a messenger. Your time is up, Walter. They've made a decision at last. An all-night meeting. A compromise solution was suggested which, though not ideal, did not damage the long-term objectives of either party. There's a place for you now. Provision has been made. Your er...loyalty to this company, and all-round contribution to society, albeit in the narrow area of bread mass production, served you well. The committee actually calculated how many loaves you've mixed in the forty-five years you've worked here. Two hundred and twenty million. That's an awful lot of toast Walter. They're very pleased with you. All that bread! Ha! It's a mountain Walter! The decision, in the end, was unanimous – a very rare thing. The committee are already discussing the merits of another case. Walter, trust me, it's not as terrible as it sounds. I know where you're going. It's not perfect, but it could be worse. Let's just say, there are more ovens here – *comprenez*?

You are going to die Walter. Tonight. It'll be quick, and, thankfully, there'll be hardly any mess.

Available in *Toast*, published by Oberon Books Ltd. Reprinted by kind permission of the publisher.

ISBN: 1 84002 104 7

DEAD MAN'S HANDLE

by John Constable

Dead Man's Handle was first performed by the Soho Theatre Company.

This short play is a three-hander, set in an intensive care unit where a man lies dying. The doctor is talking to the woman, who is in shock. The doctor hands her a glass of water.

Accent: any.

DOCTOR: It's okay…I don't mean… I mean I…I don't think…I don't think what you're going through is ever easy…for anyone. I have to say, I do think you're coping remarkably well.

But – oh, I think you are. But I think – I mean I don't think anyone can go through what you're going through and hold it all…you know…you've got to – got to – cry for him and… give yourself time to think it through – start to – come to terms…and I think it's good that – that's what you're starting to do. I do think…if we're going to – talk it through…I er…I think you'd better sit down.

He offers her the bedside chair. The WOMAN seems not to notice, staring at the MAN in bed. The DOCTOR coughs.

As I said, we're going to have to look at the scans in more detail. But – I'm afraid it does – does look as if there is very severe and extensive damage to his brain. Now, what this means…we can keep him alive, in a stable condition but…the fact is…that to all intents and purposes – the only things keeping his heart beating and – that sort of thing… are the drugs and the – the fact that he's on the ventilator.

The thing is…as things stand…the most we can do is – is to maintain him in some sort of – half-life. In this sense we – as doctors – we can't heal him…we're reduced to – we're really no more than…technicians…

I know it's hard – when you care for someone – even if they don't know you exist…it's – as if you – you somehow invest them with life. But — as I said – it does – does look as though the damage is irreversible. Okay?

I do think…we do have to – face the fact – he isn't going to get any better. Sooner or later I think we're going to have to – you know – to…think through some very hard…things… I think. Okay?

Available in *John Constable: Sha-Manic Plays*, published by Oberon Books Ltd. Reprinted by kind permission of the publisher.

ISBN: 1 870259 90 4

THE SNOW PALACE

by Pam Gems

The Snow Palace was first performed at the Wilde Theatre, Bracknell in January 1998 and subsequently at the Tricycle Theatre, Kilburn after a national tour.

Poland in the 1920s. In a freezing wooden hut the writer Stanislawa Przybyszewska lives alone as she writes her epic play, 'The Danton Affair', about the rivalry and jockeying for power of Danton and Robespierre during the French Revolution. Her morphine addiction causes the characters to come to life in her head, and in her hut. Here Robespierre is at the Paris Tribunal, fighting for his own survival and the destruction of his enemy, Danton. Robespierre is a fanatic and an idealist, more excited by ideas than by emotions.

Accent: received pronunciation

ROBESPIERRE: (*Shrill, against the noise.*) I request the right to speak…I request the right to speak! (*He stands, immobile, waits a long time for the noise to die down.*)

(*Mildly.*) It's a long time, gentlemen, since we began our sitting with such a display of temper. (*He pauses, looks around.*) Today…today we shall see what we value more – the Republic – or the individual.

Citizen Legendre demands that the accused be allowed to answer charges from this floor. (*Shouts of agreement. He raises his voice.*) Are you saying – are you saying that you wish to accord to those now under arrest privileges that have been denied those preceding them? If Citizen Legendre believes in special consideration then that is a mistake which we must correct in him. It is not the function of a revolutionary Convention to grant privilege. That is what we are here to abolish.

Gentlemen – what are we here for? We are here to create a new society. A society based on the notion of democracy. On the notion of personal freedom – (*A sudden scream.*) No man is born a slave! Another man makes him so! (*Some cheering. He recovers his coolness.*) We mean to build a state without hierarchy, where notions of comfort, dignity and personal happiness are not confined to the few at the expense of the many. You think that impossible? With so much energy locked in want and despair? Wasted in human beings deprived of the means of survival, let alone education, civilisation! I tell you, we have the means to unlock that energy. Here, for the first time in the history of the world, we have a chance to save the world, for the world…for the people of the world…ALL people…everywhere! Must that great work be put at risk? For personal greed? For criminality? I, Maximilien Robespierre – Citizen – say NO!!! (*Cheers.*)

I move that the order for the arrest of the prisoner Danton and his confederates be confirmed.

Available in *The Snow Palace*, published by Oberon Books Ltd. Reprinted by kind permission of the publisher.

ISBN: 1 84002 065 2

PLAYING SINATRA

by Bernard Kops

See note on the play on page 67.

Norman, an agoraphobic bookbinder with an obsessive, exclusive relationship with his sister Sandra, is trying to make her see that the man she has brought into their lives, Phillip, is a con man. It is Norman's birthday.

Accent: any.

NORMAN: Sandra darling. Let's start the party now. Please. We have to wait for no-one. That trifle looks too inviting.

(*He sits down, puts on a paper hat, smiles, leans across and puts one on her head.*) Let's start, please. I love just the two of us. (*He starts to sing 'Happy Birthday'.*) Sandra, I don't want people. I have no vacancies. I am all full up with people. Take some trifle. Don't wanna wait.

I don't think he'll be coming. (*Ending his song.*) Happy birthday to me. Who is this Phillip? Where did he come from? We know nothing about him. (*Singing to the tune 'Who Is Silvia'.*) 'Who is Phillip? What is he? That comes from outer darkness…' Sorry. If he were the good King Arthur I would fear him. I fear any stranger except Mr Frank Sinatra, but then, he's no stranger.

(*Quietly.*) Sandra! Five thousand pounds withdrawn? Yesterday? Look! This is an entry in your own little Building Society book. There! Five thousand pounds withdrawn. What have you done with the money? Or did Minerva cost that much? Has your love for me gone completely overboard? (*Now heavy*.) WHAT HAVE YOU DONE WITH THE MONEY? (*He holds her wrists, is hurting her*.) Tell me or I swear I'll murder you. What have you done with that money?

Darling! Please!

Sandra, you and I – we don't have a separate existence. If we are not us who are we then? What have all the years meant? Nothing? Am I nothing? I feel so sorry for you.

I've had enough. Think I need you? All my life you've used me as an excuse for your own fears, because you think you're as ugly as a turd. But now you've gone too far.

Not interested. Sorry Sandra. Argument over. Let's be friends. (*He goes to the table, eats voraciously*.) Try some of these cakes. They're absolutely scrumptious. Mmmmm! Sandra, I'm saying this in the nicest possible way, in a spirit of conciliation. You fell for the oldest trick in the world. You of all people. You fell for a pathetic con man, didn't you? You just gave him that money. Admit! Admit. Anyway, it's not really your fault. That's the whole point about con men; they're so believable.

Available in *Bernard Kops: Plays One*, published by Oberon Books Ltd. Reprinted by kind permission of the publisher.

ISBN: 1 84002 071 7

THE DRAMATIC ATTITUDES
OF MISS FANNY KEMBLE

by Claire Luckham

The Dramatic Attitudes of Miss Fanny Kemble was first performed at the Nuffield Theatre, Southampton in November 1990.

The play concerns the adventures of a nineteenth-century actress and darling of the West End stage, Fanny Kemble, who fell in love with and married a wealthy American landowner, Pierce Butler. Pierce owns plantations and therefore slaves, and he is greatly distressed and his life upset when his new wife takes the side of the slaves over her husband's interests. Here he is trying to make Fanny 'see sense' about the slaves.

Accent : Southern American.

PIERCE: Imagine any damn thing you like! You're an actress, Fanny, you are trained to use your imagination in the theatre, on stage. There's no place for all this feverish imagining in real life. I've got to run this place – and run this place I will, with or without your help.

You're making my job practically impossible. Dramatising everything, the whole damn time. You can't help it. It's in your blood.

Go on, make a scene, make me feel like a worm. I've attacked the precious family.

I am sick to death with you and your imagination. People have dogs that they imagine are human. I like dogs, and their owners can be my best friends. But a dog is a dog.

They only think they are human because they spend all
their time giving them human characteristics; reading all
manner of bosh into a doggy nature, simply because the
blasted dog can't answer back. I mean the dog would say
it was a dog if it could! It is the same – you think that they
can't talk to you on your level because they haven't got the
culture, rather the education. But we have education,
letters, music, art – culture – because we're white. It's
happened because we've made it happen.

I am a practical person, and I know that the only way to
deal with my slaves is to treat them in a disciplined,
sensible manner. While you! I can't have you going around
treating them as though they were martyrs, some kind of
superior being.

Frightened? I'm not frightened. Look, Fanny, I've given
you everything you've asked for. I'm loving, understanding,
generous – to a fault. All I'm asking is that you stay out of
this. Frightened? What the hell of?

I'm going to change for dinner before you say anything
else. This is absurd.

Available in *Luckham: Plays*, published by Oberon Books
Ltd. Reprinted by kind permission of the publisher.

ISBN: 1 870259 68 8

YO-YO

by Dino Mahoney

See note on the play and plot outline on page 27.

Kevin, a divorced schoolteacher, has arrived in Cornwall expecting to spend some time with his infant son, Ben. Kevin is aged thirty, a secondary school teacher working in London. He has working class origins, and is university educated. Kevin's life is invaded by Lego, a troubled fourteen-year-old boy, who is determined to gain his attention. Their relationship develops in unexpected directions as both man and boy discover some sense of kindred with each other. Kevin is talking to Lego.

Accent : London.

KEVIN: (*Spluttering with laughter.*) I don't know. I have nothing to laugh about Lego...nothing. (*He again splutters with laughter.*) It's hysteria, take no notice... (*He drinks.*) I was doing volcanoes once.

There I was at the blackboard...coloured chalks...sound effects... (*Mimes chalking up an erupting volcano with appropriate sound effects.*) all accompanied by a riveting commentary on the earth's pent up energies...the trapped lava seething below the earth's crust...gripping stuff...then all aglow I turn around and see this slob in the front row sprawling at his desk with a lolly rammed down his throat, the stick poking out of his mouth...so I grab it and pull.

It was like yanking the pin out of a hand grenade. He put his fist through the door...it had glass panels in it... reinforced glass, you know the kind...chicken wire in it...well, it's that kind of school, they reinforced the glass case someone put their fist through it...it's what you call...foresight. (*Pause.*) Should have been my face

Was I scared? For him, yes…for me? I think so.

We're all nutters Lego, all of us. (*He drinks*.) Went home with bloodstains on my jacket…it looked as if I worked in an abattoir…and sometimes I think I do.

What I do isn't really teaching Lego…it's more like surviving. When the morning bell goes everything human goes with it. They don't know me…I'm someone else… someone in their way…a policeman…a parent… a schoolteacher…and they swear at me, insult me, ignore me…until now I hate them back. It's pathetic.

Teach in a posh school? Ah yes…leave your ideals on the pavement Sir and step inside…no, they wouldn't have me Lego…not after seven years in the hole I've been teaching in.

Available in *Yo-Yo*, published by Oberon Books Ltd. Reprinted by kind permission of the publisher.

ISBN: 1 870259 50 5

ROOM TO LET

by Paul Tucker

Room to Let was first performed at the Chelsea Theatre Centre in May 1999.

The play is set in the living room of a terraced house that has not been decorated in years. Eddie and Janet are an ordinary couple, in their fifties, enjoying simple daily pleasures. Then they take in a lodger – Roger. Roger is thirty-three, from Swansea in South Wales. He is dressed in a feathery ginger-blond wig and a cheap second-hand sweater tucked into ill-fitting Farah hopsack trousers which are short in length. He wears eighties winklepickers with white socks. All this is topped off with a Swansea FC tattoo on one forearm and 'Mother' on the other. Together with the tinted glasses and the moustache, he thinks he's cool and trendy, the man about town. Roger is, in fact, Eddie's son from a previous marriage. Eddie abandoned them when Roger was a small baby. Here, Roger confronts Eddie about the pain he has caused.

Accent : South Wales.

ROGER: You'll never be able to make up for what you've done. At school, the kids called me a bastard, I used to dread it, walking through those big black metal gates in the morning where they would be waiting for me, the sky would be yellow and grey and you wunt believe how low I was for a nine-year-old. They would tear my hood off my coat or hit me with their belts when the teacher wasn't there, or they'd gob in my face or make me lie in dogshit, if they didn't call me a bastard, they called me flea bag or lurgy or leper. Mum couldn't afford new clothes so I never told her about the rips in my trousers or in my coat, I would sit in my bedroom and sew them up myself. Every day, I thought you might come back, I would imagine you walk up that garden path and you'd look up and see me at the bedroom window and as you'd come through that front door, things would be normal again. The sun would come back, Christmas would be a time to look forward to and I would never have to hear mam crying downstairs all the time and listening to that song every five minutes. But you never came did you? You never walked up that path did you? You just walked right out of our lives, gone, as if you never existed, as if we didn't either. I wanted to find you, I wanted to see what you had to say, it was heart-breaking to watch her die, it killed me Eddie, it really fucking killed me. And where were you? You weren't by her bedside, you weren't holding her hand, you weren't telling her everything's gonna be okay and God'll look after her. But the more hurt I felt then, the more I would make you pay, and now I don't have to cry any more. Because it's your turn now, Eddie, it's your turn to do the crying.

Available in *Room to Let*, published by Oberon Books Ltd. Reprinted by kind permission of the publisher.

ISBN: 1 84002 125 X